CUPID'S RAGE

Also by Laala Kashef Alghata

Friendship in Knots
Behind the Mask: A Folded Heart

Cupid's Rage

Laala Kashef Alghata

First published in 2015 by
Gulf International Publications
P O Box 10865
Manama
Bahrain

Text copyright © 2015 Laala Kashef Alghata
Cover illustration copyright © 2015 Carina Santos

The moral rights of the author and cover illustrator have been
asserted.

L.D. 2015 / د.ع / 479
ISBN 978-99901-10-79-1

First Edition

Limited No. 67 of 200

Printed and bound in Bahrain

Table of Contents

i.

My Soul is a Hidden Orchestra 11
Sixth Sense 12
Replaced 13
Cupid's Rage 14
Sweetheart, 15
Swollen Lips 16
Sometimes 17
They Say, Hope 18
As They Do 19
Like Thunder 22
A Poet's Search for Her Soul 23
Dali's Rose 24
I Want to Feel Van Gogh's Night 25
The Painters and I 26

ii.

Regard Me Sadly 31
Neighbours 33
Glaswegian Night 34
Wax and Wane 35
Ashes to Ashes 36
The End of the Beginning 37
Wild 38
Heat Crawled Past 40
Birth of Days 41
Roadside Flowers 42
Green Fields 43
One Man 45

Acknowledgements 49

j

My Soul is a Hidden Orchestra
Title quoted from Fernando Pessoa

If your soul were an orchestra,
I'd want to be the entire trumpet section,
play my way into your heart (and take a piece
as a keepsake), dabble in your mind,
anchor myself in the notes swimming
in your blood.

If my soul were an orchestra,
I'd want you to take over
as conductor, and as you perform
every part of me would sing,
and my pen would dance without me.

Sixth Sense

Love is the burnt soles of summer,
how we hurt ourselves hurrying
to get nowhere quickly, the inflamed
skin, the flush pink of our heels.

It is nerves and optical fibres,
umbilical cords linked to our nervous
system. Love is a sixth sense,
a whisper down your spine
that grips your tailbone.

Love is a highway mirage,
a shimmer that teases hope,
fading as you approach.

Replaced

I let your words spin
around my mouth like a Ferris wheel.
The ride goes on.

I watch you, your murky eyes,
the hard edge of your lips,
the ready fist at your side.

Your words dissolve,
slide down, replaced.
The wheel goes on.

Cupid's Rage

Wrap your arms around me,
make me feel your forgotten love.
Kiss me slowly, tenderly; let me know
how to sense that vibrant,
fading rainbow.

Let me rest in my clichés
and recall every single night
with all of Cupid's rage,
when we fell for the wrong one.

Let us fall: broken, entwined,
a modern pair of star-fucked lovers.

Press this thorn into my cornea
if you remember a time
when I once called you
the apple of my eye.

Sweetheart,

tell me your fantasies
and exactly how many
I'm in.

Sweetheart,
grab me
and do what you wish.
I know how to stop you
and when.

Sweetheart,
lean past your fucking defences.
Tell them how you lied,
how you love me.

Sweetheart,
some more of me is waiting
when you turn the page—

Swollen Lips

You'd think we have written love out
enough. That we'd leave that topic
well enough alone. Move on

past thighs and broken hearts
and touch our swollen lips goodbye.

Sometimes
Inspired by Lisa Zaran

Sometimes
I like being under the covers
alone.

Sometimes
I want you there beside me.

Sometimes
I want you to be
the shoulder I cry on.

Sometimes
I wonder if I ever loved you
the way I know I did.

Sometimes
I wish I could hit you
harder.

Sometimes
death washes over me
like a breeze.

They Say, Hope

When we reach
the end of the rope,
we turn to the wise

and they say, *have hope.*
Like it's the easiest thing
to keep a hold of, forgetting
hope is slippery.

They say, *have hope.*
Like it is abundant,
a field of dandelions floating
in the breeze.

They say, *have hope.*
Like it's something
you can have servings of,
a spoonful with every meal.

They say, *have hope.*
Like it's something
they're offering us.

As They Do

i.

Behind the ebony of our destruction
music plays in our ears,
your grassy eyes are soft
with tears,
vying for redemption.

Immerse yourself in my heart's azure
drink every drop
drink it dry

and find what it is
in that barren land
that keeps on
churning,
churning.

Before the ebony of our destruction
before you leave, as they do,
listen to the music in our ears
let it seep inside,
trust in hope

to stop my chocolate eyes
from sinking

or drink every drop
drink it dry.

ii.

She hides behind the shattered fragments
of that golden lily
eating pollen to survive.

They left her, as they do,
perched on the tip of a tree-branch,
reaching for the ground

instead of the sky,
hunting for the feeling
of something solid
underneath her feet

instead of reaching high
and realising dreams.

She curls around herself
(she is her own parenthesis)
enveloped in emptiness
and a shattered lily blanket.

iii.

The smoke rising
from a stranger's abandoned cigarette
blurs your face. You are in remission,
making a slow retreat

after wrecking through
my heart.

You place your blackened fingers
in the soft hollow
of feeling
where I swallow.
You shift your attention,
your mind in disarray.

The grassy green of your eyes
bleed and your iris is blank,
a white canvas
or a Chinese man's funeral robes.

You plug the emptiness
and I'm flooded
with warmth
(don't drink this,
lay me down to bathe).

You dissolve, as memories do.
Your name brushes past my lips
and rots, nestled, in my heart.

Like Thunder

I told the world to cry diamonds
because that's how much pain is worth
and as your eyes drop I catch a gem,
note its radiance, 1.28 carats
of distress resting in my hand like thunder.

I smile into your mouth, my remedy
to your every malady, let my eyes
scream laughter and let my gaze fall
on you. You tilt your head back
and I bow my body down.

I take your fingers in mine and between
us we're clasping your soul so tightly
it begins to bleed. You say, look how I hurt.

I say, yes, but most wisdom stems from pain.

A Poet's Search for Her Soul

Your lips are powder blue
on my soul. I try to brush away
the kisses but they are plunged
into my heart like Excalibur.

I let you poke your fingers in
between my heart and my lungs,
squeezing all the way. It is in this way
I fell in and out of love
and lost my breath when I saw you.

All the while I'm wondering
where exactly it is the soul resides
and how many times we have to fall
in love to find it.

Dali's Rose

Inspired by Dali's Rose Meditative

The rose hangs in the air,
in the balance of probability,
bleeding beauty gently
into its surroundings.
Whomever loved
that loved not at first sight?

Stemless, its petals fold back.
I want to climb into its womb
and dissolve in its softness,
forget the world, hovering
in the sky with no visible means
of support.

There is a drop on the petal's lip
and my cheeks are wet.

I Want to Feel Van Gogh's Night

Like swirls wrapped tightly around me
and how comfort can be blue,
and black spikes are not always evil,
I want to kiss the night.

Like his strokes, so crude
and the city, so quiet,
I want merge—
                    crude and noisy.

The stars, so yellow,
each its own sun
and how his night is light,
but the people sleep.

I want to feel Van Gogh's night,
I want to sleep bathed in light.

The Painters and I

i.

Michelangelo would be afraid to paint
my portrait, if he were asked,
he would say, *no;* shake his head then
repeat, *no.*

Michelangelo would be afraid to paint
my portrait, for he'd see the hunger
in my lips, slightly cracking but flushed pink
and the loneliness in my eyes,
he would understand chocolate brown
is not always warm.

I see the dejectedness in your posture,
he'd mutter, *I cannot paint what I do not
want to preserve. You're lost,* he'd whisper.
I paint those who are found.

ii.

Picasso would tilt his head if asked
to paint my portrait. He'd try
and sit me down, move my arms.
He'd look at me intently, his expression
clear; I am what cubists look for,
broken before they even paint.

iii.

Warhol would not be convinced
to paint my picture. *You are not famous,*
he'd say, *you are no one.*

If Warhol could be convinced
to paint me, my lips would be
smudged more than his Monroe,
as would my eyes. He'd hide my soul
in his work. He'd hide me.

iv.

If I were asked to paint myself
and I have been, I would do it
in oil pastel, smudge myself
with ridiculous colours, greens
and oranges and reds.

You make yourself look an alien,
they exclaim,

and I say, *exactly.*

Regard Me Sadly

"People or stars
Regard me sadly, I disappoint them," Sylvia Plath, Sheep
in Fog

The stars nestle deeper
into the sky, throwing
occasional light my way,
sometime-brightness,
sometime-beauty.

From their fixed places,
from their warmth,
they judge me with sad hearts,
diminish themselves
as I am not worthy
of their magnificence.

The stars nestle deeper
into the sky, on the brink
of disappearing,
as I hurtle further away
from expectations.

I wish to steal the wisdom
of their hearts and step
on the sadness in their eyes
until it is flattened and gone.

The stars regard me sadly,
whispering in comets
across the skies, reaching heaven
with their distress.

Neighbours

Hidden in the silence of surrender,
your love disappeared. Little white circles
that dance, a jig my mind remembers.
My hands a warm crater, they melted
in the heat of your defeat. You ran
as far as the world would let you. White
corners in estates – my eyes slip past
Gothic architecture. The cathedral ruins
stand taller than me – even as I stretch my arms and
push myself up. I cannot push past the sky.
It is too near. The stars are my neighbours,
I shout at the comets to be quiet and not leave
a trail in my backyard. The northern lights
are my distant cousins; they keep themselves
where their splendour will not fade. I furrow
myself into the ground. The cloud's tears collapse
my lungs and my heart is breathing.

Glaswegian Night

Your memory hangs about
my silhouette, like laughter.
Your eyes, darker than a Glaswegian night,
shone brightly. I saw the tears,
reflected them in my own
and said nothing.

Our fingers intertwined
across the miles. Your breath hot
against my cheek, your smile waning.
You ate apples and let the cores
fall at your feet.

Wax and Wane

The stars shake. The sky skims
the ocean and comes back up
            sharply
falling back onto the breeze.

The edges rattle.

The world stirs, the ground splits
and infinity leaps out, a prisoner.
The clouds gather and attack,
the sea begins its advance.

Like seeds in oil, the sun burns and explodes.

Ashes to Ashes

Stardust glimmers patterns
of eternity along a moonlit sky,
falling in loops and curves
at my feet, fearing seclusion.

The night turns ashes of grey,
colour failing this, the ceiling
of our thoughts, the moon
a crescent bubbling behind
the charcoal clouds.

Hope flees this battle scene,
joy runs fast on its heel
as despair murmurs, blowing
softy on my mind.

The End of the Beginning

Darkness licks at my heels
and I surrender,
waving the black flag
of my home, my body,
letting the depression laze
around my person
like a shimmer.

Memory works wonders
we despise,
knitting nightmares
into the very fabric
of our hearts.

With each end a new beginning,
so, then, one must come—
waving its white flag cheerily,
running along the shore.

Wild

It was a first. Outside the landscape lay
dirty, drenched, white. We walked,
the world seeping into our boots,
our laughter spilling over:
honey
        or jam, dripping sloppily
        falling like blood
                or berries
your chuckle escaped in a hiss,
flavoured the air, rose in steam,
caressing my cheek. My giggles
were crass, uncontrolled, wild.
        He didn't like it—
                You whispered,
                so what?
and I laughed,
to their chagrin.

The world was what it is:
a cover, an illusion. Your eyes
in the sunlight
                hazy, pale,
        like the moon
                (or something
        less predictable, you said).
Like the moon, I insist. Full
of holes and craters. A hint
of a soul in its depths.

The sun hid behind the clouds.

Your eyes shone, bright
and disorienting. Always
a paradox, I said.
Not always,
you whisper.

Heat Crawled Past

His hands lay dormant.
She spoke to him of patterns and stardust,
made him lie next to her in the dark
as the heat crawled past them,
howling at the moon
and provoking the sky.

The land dripped with sweat,
windows stained with its salt.

His eyes erupt. The sun does not
rise, and sudden stillness suffocates.
She dances by the wayside, writhing
in ecstasy. His eyes hold her, spitting ash.

Darkness hovers, waiting for the sky
to shed skins. Twilight dances in the breeze.

Her heart lay dormant.
She tattoos its likeness on her skin
and takes his hand in hers – her lips erupt
with fervour and meet his eyes.

The sun appears, frozen on the horizon.

Birth of Days

He pushed her away,
hid his eyes, choked on being alone.

Her heart broke trying
to fall in step with his.
His arm shook, a nervous tick,
his watch ticked, his throat dry.
He didn't know Joy didn't come
painted on the side of the box.

She forgot everything
but the dove shaped mark
on his shoulder.
He kept running closer,
then sprinting away.

Her lips part to scream anger
but they form a soft kiss instead
(on a stranger's face, his hands,
his groin), she screams
herself hoarse.

She pulls him closer,
his soft blue shirt
between her legs.

Roadside Flowers

He stands by the side of the road,
his arms draped with jasmine chains,
wearing a button-up shirt unbuttoned
and exhaustion in his eyes.

His friend sells roses
long stems, offering up love
or maybe just a chance.

The heat slides over them,
like blindness, dizziness and dehydration.
They wipe the sweat from their brown skin
offer a flower for a dinar,
something to decay,
fill the car with summer smells.

Bloom at night, fill the house
with flowers, slip them a note —
and barter, two perhaps, for one?
And one retreats, depleted.

The other does not even shrug,
hands over his bounty,
slips the half-note in his pocket
weaves between the cars,
vying for another quick purchase
bathed in the glow of the traffic light's red.

No hope, no future, just routine.
The cars drive toward the green.

Green Fields

i.

I associate green with death.
I have never seen someone
die, though I have watched
the slow decay of souls

and their hands, white knuckles
clawing at Life, trying to hang on
on this side of it all, spitting
at the angel of death.

When he died, I arrived seconds
after the undertaker left.
I never saw his body, but
the destruction

in his wake was palpable,
his wife in a corner, back stiff,
cheeks as dry as the Sahara sun
as her daughter grabbed

at the air, trying to anchor his soul
in the Amazon of her tears.

ii.

My father's voice on the line.

I thought we still had time—
he didn't tell me that it was
done — it was over —

so I dressed to watch death arrive.

All I saw was a green poster
fluttering on the wall. His sheets
pulled over his body, a lump of white.
My face a home for the Amazon

and the cries rising in crescendo
as they lifted him
up, up and away.

One Man

It's easy to forget the dead
once time has passed. Moments
you thought would be engraved
in your memory erode, details
washed away. I forgot his eyes—

unlike any other I've seen,
light grey and blue. Beautiful eyes,
which cupped a spark.
I don't know I could forget
his eyes, or his laugh

and the way he held out his hand
when I would kiss him hello.

When I knew him, his face
was weathered. Old and wrinkled,
as handsome as ever. A smile
splitting open his mouth,
languages spilling out

Arabic, English, Urdu, Persian.
One man, four tongues, which he passed
onto us. My two tongues split
in an effort to be four. They fail
and curl up in defeat.

For half a second I forgot
his eyes, but my toe still curls
the way his did.

Acknowledgements

Thanks to the editors of the following publications, where some of these poems first appeared:
Contemporary American Voices
The Peregrine Muse
All Things Girl
Write Me a Metaphor

Thanks especially to Patty Paine, Jeff Lodge and Samia Touati for selecting *Regard Me Sadly* and *Roadside Flowers* for Gathering the Tide, an anthology of contemporary Arabian Gulf poetry. The anthology and its launch was a singular event on the Gulf poetry scene and it was a pleasure to be a part of it.

Thank you also to Deborah Pagano, co-founder of the Clemson Arts Centre in South Carolina, US who used *I Want To Feel Van Gogh's Night* as the focus of a month-long exhibition. Twenty-five artists were asked to interpret the poem on canvas, while visitors were encouraged to write a poem or draw a picture inspired by the poem on white cards that hung from the ceiling. The interactive exhibition it resulted in was wonderful and a real joy to witness.

Finally, thank you to Carly Brown for her efforts in looking over these poems and to Carina Santos for creating the wonderful cover.

Laala Kashef Alghata (b. 1990) is an Iraqi-Bahraini poet. She currently works as a journalist in Bahrain. Her debut, a middle-grade novel called Friendship in Knots, made her the first Bahraini to publish a book in English and, at 13, the youngest (at the time) to publish a book. Her second book, a poetry and prose collection, Behind the Mask: A Folded Heart, was published in 2006.

For more information, visit www.laala.co